THE
EMPTY TOMB

Text copyright © 2008 Brian Sibley
Illustrations copyright © 2008 Stephen Waterhouse
This edition copyright © 2023 Lion Hudson IP Limited

Lion Children's Books
Part of the SPCK Group
SPCK, Studio 101, The Record Hall, 16-16A Baldwins Gardens,
London, EC1N 7RJ

ISBN 978 0 7459 7974 8

1 3 5 7 9 10 8 6 4 2

Stories first published in 2008 in *50 Favourite Bible Stories*

A catalogue record for this book is available from the British Library

First printed in China by Dream Colour (Hong Kong) Printing Ltd

Produced on paper from sustainable forests

THE
EMPTY TOMB

A STORY OF EASTER

Retold by **BRIAN** SIBLEY

Illustrated by **STEPHEN WATERHOUSE**

LION
CHILDREN'S

INTRODUCTION

From the moment of Jesus' birth, which we remember and celebrate every Christmas, his life was special. He grew up loving God, calling him 'Father', and doing what he knew God was asking him to do.

As a young man, Jesus spent his days telling people the good news about God's great love for them. He also spoke about the ways in which God wanted people to live and to care for one another.

Jesus had a group of twelve special friends, who became known as his 'disciples'. They journeyed around towns and villages. Wherever they went, Jesus helped those who were unwell or had worries. He told everyone who would listen wonderful stories, called parables, to explain the message that God wanted him to share.

Although Jesus was greatly loved for his kindness and wisdom, not everyone liked the things that he said and did. Eventually, some of those against Jesus began plotting to stop his teaching and to get rid of him. But, as you will read in this book, that is not what happened, and over two thousand years later, the story of Jesus' life is known in every corner of the world.

BRIAN SIBLEY

CONTENTS

1. RIDING TO JERUSALEM

Jesus decided to go to Jerusalem. When he was a little way off from the city, he sent two of his twelve followers on ahead of him to a village further down the road.

'When you get there,' he told them, 'you will find a donkey tied up, and beside her will be her young colt, which has not yet been ridden by anyone. Untie the animals and bring them here. And if anyone asks you what you are doing or why, simply say, "The Master needs them," and no one will do anything to stop you.'

So the two men went on ahead and everything happened exactly as Jesus had said.

When they returned, they put their coats over the back of the young donkey for Jesus to sit on. As he rode towards Jerusalem, a crowd began following him. Others ran on in front and covered the ground with their cloaks and with branches torn from the palm trees.

It was like a royal procession; the crowd grew bigger and bigger, and soon everyone was singing and chanting: 'Praise to King David's son! Praise to the man who comes in the name of the Lord God! Peace in heaven and glory to God!'

Eventually, Jesus and the crowd arrived at the gates of Jerusalem; as soon as they entered the city, the place was in uproar. 'Who *is* this man?' asked some of the people who didn't know Jesus. The crowd shouted back, 'It's Jesus, the teacher from Nazareth in Galilee!'

Some of the religious leaders grew worried at the number of people who were crowding the city streets and exciting everyone with their singing and shouting. 'Teacher,' they begged Jesus, 'tell your followers to be quiet.'

But Jesus shook his head. 'I tell you,' he said, 'even if the people were to be silent, all the stones in the walls and streets of Jerusalem would start shouting!'

When the procession reached the Temple, Jesus got off the donkey and went inside.

What he saw upset him very much. Everywhere he looked, there were people exchanging money and buying and selling birds and animals for sacrifices. It was more like a market than a place where people go to worship God.

Jesus became so angry that he began knocking over the traders' tables. Within minutes, there were coins rolling all over the Temple floor and the air was full of pigeons flying up from the cages that had smashed open when they hit the ground.

In a loud voice, Jesus called out, 'God said, "My Temple will be called a house of prayer," but you are making it into a hideout for thieves!'

The religious leaders were very angry that Jesus had done this, but the ordinary people flocked into the Temple to listen to Jesus speak and brought friends and family who were unwell so that he could make them better.

2. THE LAST SUPPER

Each day after he arrived in Jerusalem, Jesus went to the Temple to teach; every evening, he went up onto the Mount of Olives to be alone with God.

Some of the priests and religious leaders believed that Jesus was a dangerous troublemaker, and they began plotting to get rid of him, although they didn't dare do anything when Jesus was in the Temple surrounded by crowds of people.

Then someone unexpected offered to help Jesus' enemies. One of Jesus' twelve followers, Judas Iscariot, agreed to hand Jesus over to them, and when they promised to pay him money, he began looking for an opportunity to betray Jesus.

It was time for celebrating the festival of Passover, when the Jewish people remember how God had led them out of slavery in Egypt.

Jesus and the twelve followers met to eat the Passover meal in an upstairs room. When they were sitting at the table, Jesus said, 'I have wanted so much to eat this meal with you before I suffer.'

His followers were wondering what he meant, when he told them something that shocked them even more.

'One of you,' said Jesus looking round the table, 'will betray me.'

They all began talking at once. 'Who?' they asked. 'It's not me, is it?' The last to ask was Judas. 'Surely, Teacher,' he said, 'you don't mean *me*?'

Jesus simply answered, 'So you say.'

Then Jesus said a prayer of thanks to God for the meal they were about to eat. Taking the bread, he broke it and handed it to the others. 'Take and eat it,' he said. 'This is my body.'

When they had shared the bread, Jesus took a cup of wine and, after another prayer of thanks, handed it to his followers to be passed around.

'Drink it, all of you,' he said. 'This is my blood, which guarantees God's promise to forgive people for all the wrongs they have done.'

When the meal was finished, all of them except Judas went with Jesus to the Mount of Olives.

On the way, Jesus began telling his friends things that, at the time, they didn't understand. 'This very night,' he said, 'all of you will run away and leave me.'

Peter was quick to reply. 'I will *never* leave you!' he said firmly. 'Even if all the others do, I never shall!'

Jesus looked Peter in the eyes. 'I tell you, Peter,' he said, 'before the cock crows, you will say three times that you do not even know me.'

Peter was hurt. 'I will never say that,' he said angrily, 'even if I have to die with you!'

When they reached a garden called Gethsemane, on the Mount of Olives, Jesus told his followers to sit and wait for him. Taking Peter, James and John, he walked further on.

'I am very sad,' Jesus told his three friends, 'and I feel as if I am being crushed by my unhappiness. Please stay close by and keep watch while I pray to my Father.'

Jesus went on a little way alone and knelt down. 'Father,' he prayed, 'I feel as if I were being offered a drink from a cup that is full of pain and suffering.'

Then, in tears, Jesus asked, 'If it is possible, Father, please do not let me be handed this cup. But if it is what you want to happen, then I will do as you ask.'

Jesus talked with God for an hour, and when he came back, he found Peter, James and John sound asleep with tiredness and worry.

'Wake up!' he called. 'Could you not keep awake for just one hour?'

His friends were upset. 'You mean well in your hearts,' said Jesus, 'but the human body is weak. Ask God to keep you from giving way to temptation. Come now, it is time to go.'

And as he spoke, they saw a lot of people with burning torches making their way up the path towards the garden.

3. THE CRUCIFIXION

Judas arrived in the garden of Gethsemane with some of the religious leaders and a crowd of men carrying swords and sticks. He went straight up to Jesus and kissed him.

This was the signal that the crowd had been waiting for and they immediately grabbed Jesus.

'Judas,' said Jesus, 'do you betray me with a kiss?'

Then, turning to the crowd, he said, 'Did you really have to come with weapons to catch me in the night as if I were an outlaw? I was with you every day in the Temple and you never tried to arrest me!'

Jesus was led off towards the city and, just as he had said would happen, his friends ran away. Only Peter followed, at the very back of the crowd, to see what would happen.

When they reached the house of the high priest, Peter sat down by a fire in the courtyard. While he was sitting there, first one person and then another asked if he was a friend of Jesus, but each time he said, 'No!'

The third time he was asked, Peter said, 'Listen, I've no idea what you're talking about!' But he had hardly finished speaking when a cock crowed, and he remembered that Jesus had said that he would deny knowing him three times.

In the morning, the priests and religious teachers questioned Jesus and asked him if he was the great king who had long been promised to the Jewish people.

'If I tell you,' replied Jesus, 'you will not believe me.'

'Are you the Son of God?' they demanded. Jesus answered, 'You say that I am.'

So they took Jesus to Pontius Pilate, the Roman governor, and demanded that Jesus be put to death because his claims to be the promised king would cause trouble and riots throughout the country.

Pilate asked Jesus, 'Are you the king of the Jews?' And again Jesus replied, 'So you say.'

Although Pilate didn't want to upset the religious leaders, he believed that Jesus was innocent.

Hoping to set Jesus free, Pilate took him out to the people and asked them what he should do. But the crowd was full of Jesus' enemies and they yelled at the top of their voices, '*Crucify him! Crucify him!*'

Finally, Pilate gave in and handed Jesus over to the Roman guards. They whipped him and then made fun of him by dressing him up in a purple robe and making him a crown of branches of thorn. Bowing down to him, they shouted, 'Long live the king of the Jews!'

Then the soldiers led Jesus away to a place outside the walls of Jerusalem where criminals were executed.

Jesus was nailed to a cross of wood by his hands and feet, and left to hang there until he died. Despite the terrible pain, Jesus prayed for his executioners. 'Forgive them, Father!' he called out. 'They don't know what they are doing.'

A notice was fixed to the cross saying, 'This is the king of the Jews.' Two thieves were crucified with Jesus, one on either side of him, and one of them called out, 'If you're really the Son of God, save yourself and us!'

But the other thief said, 'We deserve our punishment, but Jesus has done nothing wrong.' Then he said to Jesus, 'Remember me when you are king.'

Jesus replied, 'I promise that today you will be with me in my Father's kingdom.'

The Roman soldiers on duty at the foot of the cross gambled with dice for Jesus' clothes and many of his enemies came by to laugh at his suffering.

Storm clouds filled the sky and for three hours the sun never shone.

Among the crowd, Jesus saw his mother Mary holding on to the arm of John, who was one of his twelve followers.

Looking at them and seeing how sad they were, Jesus said, 'Mother, John is now your son. John, she is now your mother.'

And from that day, John took Mary to live in his house.

Jesus asked for a drink, so a soldier filled a sponge with wine, put it on a stick and lifted it up to his lips.

Then Jesus spoke for the last time. 'It is finished,' he said. Then he bowed his head and died.

4. THE EMPTY TOMB

As soon as Jesus had been sentenced to die, Judas realized what a terrible thing he had done and went to the religious leaders who had given him money to hand Jesus over to them.

'I have sent an innocent man to his death!' he said, and he tried to give back the thirty pieces of silver that he had been paid.

'That's your business, not ours!' the leaders replied, refusing the money.

Judas threw the coins onto the Temple floor and, deeply ashamed of what he had done, he went and hanged himself.

There was a man named Joseph who was one of the religious teachers who had cross-examined Jesus, but had disagreed with what had been done to him. After Jesus had died on the cross, Joseph went to Pontius Pilate and asked if he could take care of Jesus' body.

Pilate gave his permission, and Joseph, helped by some of Jesus' friends, including a group of women followers, took down the body from the cross and wrapped it in a linen sheet. Then they carried Jesus' body to a garden where there was a tomb carved out of the rocks – a tomb that Joseph had bought for his own burial when his time came to die.

Joseph laid the body of Jesus in the tomb, which was closed up with a large stone rolled across the entrance.

All this happened on a Friday; the next day was the Jewish holy day when nobody worked.

Very early on the Sunday morning, just as the day was dawning, the women set off for the tomb with special spices and perfumes that they had prepared to put on Jesus' body.

As they went, the women were wondering how they could get help to roll the stone away from the entrance to the tomb; but when they reached the garden, they were shocked and astonished to find that it had already been moved. The tomb was open, and when they went in, they found that it was empty.

While they were puzzling over this, two men in shining clothes appeared nearby. The women were terribly afraid and bowed down to them, wondering what it could mean.

Then the men, who were angels, spoke and asked, 'Why are you looking among the dead people for someone who is alive? Jesus is not here. He has risen!'

The women went back at once to tell the news to Jesus' eleven followers, but when the men heard the story they thought the women were talking nonsense and refused to believe them.

Peter, however, decided to go and see for himself. He ran to the garden, and when he looked inside the tomb, he saw the linen cloth that had been wrapped around Jesus' body, but no sign of Jesus.

Realizing that something very wonderful had happened, Peter went home, hardly daring to believe that what he had seen was true.

5. THE ROAD TO EMMAUS

On the day the women found the tomb empty, two of
Jesus' followers were going from Jerusalem to a village
named Emmaus.

They were talking over everything that had happened
when a stranger joined them.

'What are you talking about?' the stranger asked.

'Well,' said one of the two, named Cleopas, 'you must be the only visitor to Jerusalem who doesn't know the things that have been happening!'

'What things?' asked the man.

'About Jesus of Nazareth,' said Cleopas. 'He was a good man, loved by God and the people, and we hoped that he was the promised king; but he was treated like a criminal, sentenced to death, and crucified.'

'What's more,' added Cleopas's companion, 'this morning some of the women in our group went to where Jesus was buried and couldn't find his body. Others say they have seen his tomb and that it's empty. So now we don't know what to believe.'

The stranger looked at the two. 'You should believe that all these things happened,' he said, 'because they were meant to happen and were written about years ago by Moses and other wise men.'

As they walked, the stranger taught Cleopas and his companion many things. It was almost dark when they reached Emmaus and they persuaded the man to join them for a meal.

When they were sitting at the table, the stranger took a loaf of bread, said a blessing, and broke it into pieces. That was when they realized who he was. It was Jesus!

It was as if they had been blind and could suddenly see, but just as they recognized him, he disappeared from sight.

The two went straight back to Jerusalem to tell the others what had happened. While they were telling their story, Jesus was suddenly standing in the room with them.

'Peace be with you,' he said.

Everyone was terrified and thought that they were seeing a ghost. 'Do not be afraid!' said Jesus. 'See the wounds left by the nails. Touch me, feel me, and you will see that I am real. Ghosts are not made of flesh and bone!'

Then Jesus said, 'I have work for you all. When I am with God my Father, I will send you heavenly strength to do the things I am going to ask of you. I want you to tell everyone that I died and came back from the dead so that God would forgive all the wrong and wicked things that people have done. This is a message for the whole world and you will tell it to them.'

Then Jesus led them out of Jerusalem. When they were a little way from the city, he raised up his hands and blessed them; as he was doing so, he left them and they saw him no longer.

Then Jesus' followers returned to Jerusalem and went to the Temple to praise God and give thanks for everything that Jesus had taught them.

6. GOD'S HOLY SPIRIT

After Jesus had returned to his heavenly Father, the eleven faithful followers went back to Jerusalem. There they found a place to stay and often met with other friends of Jesus to pray. Jesus' own mother, Mary, was one of the group of more than a hundred.

There was one important thing they had to agree on together: how to replace Judas. They asked God to guide them in making the choice, and in this way picked a man named Matthias. He had been with the group since the earliest days and had heard all of Jesus' teachings.

Now once again there were twelve chosen followers. They knew that they were the ones who were going to be responsible for carrying on the work that Jesus had begun and telling the story of his life, death, and resurrection to those who had not yet heard the Good News. But they were waiting for the heavenly strength that Jesus had promised.

Fifty days after the festival of Passover came the harvest festival called Pentecost. Jerusalem was crowded with pilgrims from many different countries who had come to worship at the Temple. Jesus' followers were meeting in a house when, suddenly, everybody heard a great noise coming from the sky that sounded as if a mighty wind was blowing. The sound roared and blasted into the room and seemed to be filling the whole house.

Then everyone there saw what looked like flames of fire, spreading out and touching each of them. In that moment, the people in the room were taken over by the Holy Spirit of God and they began talking in different languages.

There was so much noise that a great crowd gathered to see what was going on. What they heard astonished them because even though they came from various parts of the world, each and every one of them heard the story of Jesus as if it were being told in their own language.

The people in the crowd were staggered and rather frightened. 'What does it mean?' they asked. 'These are ordinary folk from Galilee. They don't speak our language and we don't speak theirs, and yet we can all understand everything they are saying!'

Some people poked fun, saying, 'They've just had too much to drink!' But then Peter stood up with the other eleven followers and, in a loud voice, spoke to the crowd.

'Let me tell you what this all means,' said Peter. 'These people are not drunk – it's only nine o'clock in the morning! No! We have been filled with the Spirit of God, as was promised long ago by the writers of the holy books. This has happened so that we can tell all of you what God has done for us and for all the world.'

Then Peter went on to tell them about Jesus. 'Listen!' said Peter. 'Jesus of Nazareth was a man of God. You know this for yourselves because you heard him speak and you saw the miracles that he did. He was handed over to wicked men who crucified him, but you all killed him by letting them do it.

'So Jesus died and was buried, but God brought him back to life and we have all seen him! Now Jesus has joined his Father and we have been given God's Holy Spirit. What you see and hear today is that gift, which has now been passed on to us.

'These are the things that you must understand: God promised that he would make a king of one of David's descendants and that king was Jesus – the man you crucified.'

When the people heard this, they were very upset. 'What shall we do?' they asked.

'Each one of you,' said Peter, 'must stop doing the wrong things that you do and be baptized in the name of Jesus so that you can be forgiven for past wrongs and be given God's Holy Spirit. This is God's promise and it has been given to you and your children and to everyone, everywhere.'

That day, 3,000 people were baptized and joined Jesus' followers and friends.

Peter and the others taught in the Temple and, by the power given to them by Jesus, healed people who were sick. And every day, as the weeks went by, the number of people who believed in Jesus grew and grew.

The stories in this book are found in the Bible.

You can read more about the events of the first Easter using these Bible references:

RIDING TO JERUSALEM

The Gospel of Matthew,
Chapter 21 verses 1–17

The Gospel of Luke,
Chapter 19 verses 28–40, 45–46

THE LAST SUPPER

The Gospel of Matthew,
Chapter 26 verses 1–5, 14–46

The Gospel of Luke,
Chapter 22 verses 1–46

THE CRUCIFIXION

The Gospel of Matthew,
Chapter 26 verse 47 – Chapter 27 verse 2, 11–38, 45–56

The Gospel of Luke,
Chapter 22 verse 47 – Chapter 23 verse 5, 13–25, 32–49

The Gospel of John,
Chapter 19 verses 1–30

THE EMPTY TOMB

The Gospel of Matthew,
Chapter 27 verse 57 – Chapter 28 verse 7

The Gospel of Luke,
Chapter 23 verse 50 – Chapter 24 verse 12

The Gospel of Mark,
Chapter 15 verse 43 – Chapter 16 verse 8

THE ROAD TO EMMAUS

The Gospel of Luke,
Chapter 24 verses 13 – end

GOD'S HOLY SPIRIT

The Acts of the Apostles,
Chapter 1 verse 12 – Chapter 2 verse 42

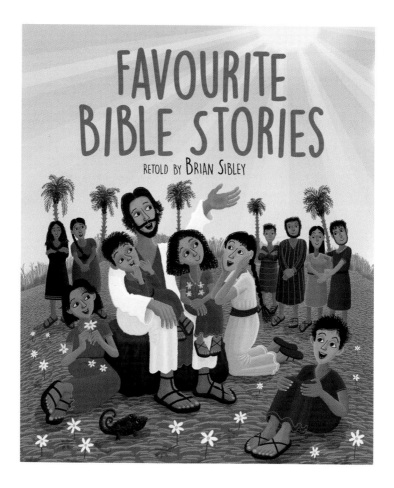

Favourite Bible Stories

Retold by Brian Sibley, illustrated by Stephen Waterhouse

Buy from: lionhudson.com/product/favourite-bible-stories

Hardback ISBN: 9780745979243